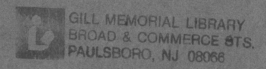

FLORENCE GRIFFITH JOYNER

APRIL KORAL

Florence Griffith JOYNER
TRACK AND FIELD STAR

FRANKLIN WATTS

A First Book

New York / London / Toronto / Sydney

To Linda Konner

Library of Congress Cataloging-in-Publication Data

Koral, April.
    Florence Griffith Joyner/April Koral.
        p. cm.—(First book)
    Includes bibliographical references and index.
    Summary: A biography of the noted sprinter who won three
gold medals at the 1988 Olympics.
    ISBN 0-531-20061-2
    1. Griffith Joyner, Florence Delorez, 1960-   —Juvenile
literature.   2. Runners (Sports)—United States—Biography—
Juvenile literature.   3. Sprinting—Juvenile literature.   4.
Olympics—Juvenile literature. [1. Griffith Joyner, Florence
Delorez, 1960-   —. 2. Runners (Sports) 3. Afro-Americans—
Biography.] I. Title. II. Series.
GV1061.15.G75K67   1992
796.42'092—dc20
[B]   91-32827 CIP AC

Contents

Chapter 1 EARLY LIFE 9

Chapter 2 THE WORLD OF TRACK 15

Chapter 3 TRAINING FOR THE OLYMPICS 21

Chapter 4 THE OLYMPIC TRIALS 37

Chapter 5 THE OLYMPIC GAMES 47

For Further Reading 62

Index 63

FLORENCE GRIFFITH JOYNER

Florence Griffith Joyner, dressed in one of her flamboyant outfits, talks to the press at the 1988 Olympic trials.

Chapter 1

IIIIEARLY LIFE

She's been called a speed queen, the First Lady of track and field, or, quite simply, the fastest woman in the world.

Florence Griffith Joyner is a sprinter—a racer who runs 100-meter and 200-meter races. She has gotten almost as much attention for her style of dressing as for her running. Most runners wear simple shorts and a T-shirt when they race. Florence Griffith Joyner has worn brightly colored one-legged tights (with the other pant leg cut off) and even bodysuits made of white lace. She likes to paint her 4-inch-long fingernails orange or red and decorate them with rhinestones or pictures of birds or trees.

But beneath the glitter, Florence Griffith Joyner is like every other successful athlete. She is dedicated, hardworking, and willing to sacrifice for a goal. Her goal has been to become a great runner. To do that, she has trained thousands of hours and pushed herself to keep going even when she was exhausted. She has also withstood pain. Most important, even after she lost races and was disappointed, Florence didn't give up. "You never fail," she says, "until you stop trying."

In the fall of 1988, at the Olympic Games in Seoul, Korea, nearly seventy thousand people jumped to their feet to cheer Florence Griffith Joyner as she dashed across the finish line to break the world record in the 200-meter dash. Newspapers and magazines hailed the 5-foot 6½-inch, 130-pound runner as the fastest woman alive. Women runners had come a long way from the time when girls were not allowed to compete in sports events in some schools. In the 1967 Boston Marathon, meet officials even tried to pull a runner out of the race after it was discovered that she was a woman.

Florence Griffith Joyner had also come a long way. She was born Delorez Florence Griffith on December 21, 1959, the seventh child in a family of six boys and five girls. Soon, everyone was calling her "Dee Dee."

Her mother, whose name was Florence also, and her father, Robert, an electronics techni-

Left: Long hours of intense training take their toll on a hardworking athlete.
Below: Florence Griffith Joyner approaches the finish line in the 1988 Olympics. After winning the 200-meter dash, she became known as "the fastest woman alive."

cian, separated when the child Florence was four years old. Her mother had no money, and moved with her children into a four-bedroom apartment in a poor area of Los Angeles called Watts.

"We had nothing," her mother once recalled. "But I explained to the children that life was like a baby. A baby comes into the world without anything. Then it starts crawling, then it stands up. Then it takes its first step and starts walking. When we moved into the housing project, I told them, 'Start walking.'"

Young Florence did more than just walk. When she was seven years old, she started going to the Sugar Ray Robinson Youth Foundation, where she became active in sports. She practiced running in local parks. She was already faster than the boys. When she would visit her father, who lived in California's Mohave Desert, she loved to chase jackrabbits.

The Griffith family was a close one, and Florence Griffith was a strict mother. During the week, the children were not allowed to watch television. Lights went out at ten o'clock. The family would get together for weekly Bible discussions that included talking about what they'd done wrong that week.

"We didn't know how poor we were," Florence has said about her early years. "We were rich as a family."

Florence became an enthusiastic reader and especially enjoyed poetry. She also kept a diary. Florence's mother was a seamstress, and her grandmother was a beautician. From them she learned how to sew and design clothing as well as to crochet. She especially liked to style hair and spent hours braiding the hair of kids in the neighborhood.

Even as a very young child, Florence was never someone who followed the crowd. Sometimes she liked to braid her hair with one braid sticking straight up. When the kids teased her, she'd just laugh with them.

Her interests were also unusual. Once, when she was in high school, she bought a boa constrictor, a type of snake, and called it Brandy. "I bathed her and lotioned her," Florence said. "Every week or two I'd go down to the pet shop and get a couple of mice or rats and feed them to her. When she shed, I saved all her skin and painted it different colors. She got to be 5 feet long. I got put out of a mall once for having her around my neck. They said people were afraid."

Florence went to Jordan High School in Watts. She won awards for sprinting and the long jump. In 1978 she graduated from Jordan and went on to college. Her most exciting, and most difficult, battle was now beginning—to win a place for herself in the history of women's track.

Chapter 2

▌▌▌▌THE WORLD OF TRACK

Florence Griffith Joyner is a champ at running 100- and 200-meter races. These races are part of the general sport of track (racing) and field (throwing and jumping). Other track events are the 400-, 800-, 1,500-, 5,000-, and 10,000-meter races and the marathon, which is 26 miles, 385 yards (42.20 kilometers) long. Field events include pole vaulting, discus and javelin throwing, and the high jump.

Runners of the short races, including, of course, the 100-meter dash, are called sprinters. What makes a great sprinter? To begin with, he or she must have excellent reflexes. The second the race begins, the sprinter must be ready to take off.

One-hundred-meter races are run in a straight line. Each runner is assigned a lane and the lanes are clearly marked by white lines. Run-

Runners, in their assigned lanes, prepare to start a race.

ners must stay in their lanes. The 200-meter race is run around an oval track, and the runners do not line up evenly in a row. That's because the runners in the outer lanes of the oval would have to run a slightly longer distance than those in the inner lanes in order to complete the race.

Before the race begins, the sprinters stand in back of the starting blocks, which are attached to adjustable metal rods. When the starter says "On your mark," the runners step forward, kneel in front of the blocks, then back their feet onto the blocks . The blocks prevent the runners' feet from slipping backward when they push forward as the race begins.

When the starter says "Set," the sprinters lift their pelvises up, ease their shoulders forward, and balance their weight between hands and front feet. They are now in position to start the race.

A few seconds later, they're off. The moment the starter's gun is fired, the athletes spring forward. If a runner moves before the gun goes off, it is called a "false start." The race is stopped and the runner receives a warning. After the first false start, a red light goes on at the foot of the block of the runner. A runner who does it again is disqualified from that race.

Above: Florence
Griffith Joyner
in position at the
starting block
Right: The starter
at the 1983 Pan
Am Games
prepares to
fire his gun.

In the Olympic Games and other major races, the pistol and the starting blocks are wired to an electronic device that can detect if a runner's foot leaves the block before the gun goes off. It is not surprising that false starts happen often. Even a fraction of a second counts in these races—so the runners are anxious to begin!

The races are timed by a clock that starts automatically when the trigger of the gun is pressed. Special equipment helps the judges determine who comes in first. A beam of light is shone across the finish line. When it is broken by the first runner who crosses it, a camera takes a picture—freezing the image on film. If there is a question of who crossed the finish line first, the judges can then look at the picture.

Because a runner's time is measured in fractions of a second, even a little wind behind the runner can make a difference, giving a tiny extra push. Judges use very sensitive devices to measure the wind. If someone runs the race in a record time but there is too much wind behind that runner, the time is not considered an official record breaker.

With or without a wind, sprinters run amazingly fast! In the first 10 meters of the 100-meter race, for example, the athlete goes from zero to

20.25 miles (32.6 kilometers) per hour! By the end of 40 to 45 meters, the runner has reached a maximum speed of about 26.1 to 26.55 miles (42–42.7 km) per hour, and maintains that speed to the end of the race.

For the 200-meter race, the sprinter tries to maintain that speed for yet another 100 meters.

Chapter 3

IIII TRAINING FOR THE OLYMPICS

In 1978, after graduating from high school, Florence went to California State University at Northridge, where she hoped to major in business. She also joined the track team.

After one year, Florence ran out of money and she had to drop out of school and get a job as a bank teller. But the assistant track coach at Northridge, Bobby Kersee, had recognized Florence's talents. He helped arrange for financial aid for her, and she returned to school. Kersee was to have a big influence on her life. When he went to the University of California at Los Angeles (UCLA) to become the coach of the women's team, Florence changed schools so that she could continue training under him. Kersee would be her coach for ten years.

For many athletes, all the work and long hours of practicing is toward one goal: competing in the Olympic Games. The Olympic Games are held once every four years, in a different host country each time. In order to be a member of the American Olympic Team, athletes compete in trials.

In 1980, when Florence was still a student at UCLA, she and her coach thought she was ready for the Olympic Games. Florence went to the trials and tried out—but she finished fourth in the 200-meter race. Another woman runner from Watts, Valerie Brisco, did make it to the Olympics. But Florence Griffith was not about to give up.

In 1982 she was the National Collegiate Athletic Association champion, running 200 meters in 22.39 seconds. In 1984 Florence tried out again for the Olympics and this time she made it. That summer she went to the Olympic Games, which were held in Los Angeles, California. She painted nine of her long fingernails red, white, and blue. One finger was painted gold—the color of the first-place medal. Florence hoped that would bring her luck. It didn't. She came in second, winning a silver medal in the 200-meter race. Her time was 22.04. First place went to Valerie Brisco.

One of the many trials Florence Griffith Joyner competed in took place at the 1982 USA/Mobil Games.

At the 1982 National Collegiate Athletic Association Games,
Florence Griffith Joyner was named NCAA champion.

Florence went home disappointed. Not only had she not won the gold but she had not even been competing against some of the world's track stars. In 1980, when the Olympics were held in Moscow, the United States had decided not to send any teams, to protest the Soviet Union's invasion of Afghanistan. Four years later, the Soviet Union, East Germany, and some other countries boycotted the Olympic Games held in the United States. Some observers wondered if Florence would have won the silver if she had been running against the well-trained women of these countries.

Florence stopped training hard; she gained 15 pounds. Her dreams of winning a gold medal at the Olympic Games seemed to be fading.

On October 10, 1987, Florence married Alfrederick Alphonzo Joyner. Al Joyner grew up in East St. Louis, Illinois. Like his wife, he is a track and field athlete. In the 1984 Olympics he won the gold medal in the triple jump. One of his two sisters is also an athlete. She is Jackie Joyner-Kersee, another great track and field athlete who would also compete in the 1988 Olympic Games. Coincidentally, Jackie is married to Bobby Kersee!

Florence Griffith Joyner (right)
and Valerie Brisco-Hooks (left) at
the 1984 Olympics held in the U.S.

Florence Griffith Joyner, Al Joyner, Jackie Joyner-Kersee,
and Bobby Kersee pose for a family photograph
after the 1988 Olympics.

In the meantime, with Kersee's encouragement, Florence had lost weight and begun to train seriously again. She had her eye on the 1987 World Championships held in Rome, Italy. The work paid off. She came in second in the 200-meter race.

The success inspired—and frustrated—her. More than ever she wanted to be number one. The Olympics were only one year away. The tryouts for the Olympics were even sooner, in July. Could she train in that time—train enough to compete against the best athletes in the world *and* come in first?

Although sprinters, like all athletes, have natural ability, they must also train their bodies for years. A great athlete cannot wake up on some mornings and say, "I don't feel like running today." Every day, athletes must spend hours strengthening their muscles and stretching their bodies to the limits of endurance.

But while she was training for the Olympics, Florence Griffith Joyner had to find a way to make money to pay her bills! Doing both was not easy.

At first, she trained at night after working all day at a bank. She also braided hair occasionally to earn extra money. Later, she got a job

The World Championships women's 4×100-meter relay
team at the games held in Rome, Italy, in 1987.
Florence Griffith Joyner is second from the right.

Florence's husband and coach, Al Joyner,
spent long hours working with her
in preparation for the Olympics.

in a company that had a special program for Olympic hopefuls. Florence was allowed to work only four hours a day so that she could have more free time to train. Still, the days were exhausting, since she often worked on the track until midnight.

Florence's workout included an hour and a half in the weight room. She used special machines that helped build up the muscles in her legs. The more powerful sprinters' upper leg muscles are, the more strength and speed they will have when they push off the blocks.

Of course, Florence also did a lot of track workouts. In addition to practicing 100- and 200-meter sprints, she also ran 3.7 miles (6 km) a day. Many coaches do not believe that sprinters should run such long distances—but Florence Griffith Joyner had her own ideas.

Besides developing their leg muscles, sprinters must train the rest of their bodies. When they run, they cannot do it wildly. A great sprinter does not waste one body movement. Every motion of the body and even the position of the arms, hands, and feet must help the sprinter move forward. When a sprinter runs, the knees lift up high (the higher the leg goes, the more force it has on the way down) and the arms swing

Florence's hours of working with weights to build up her leg muscles are evident here.

For an athlete like Florence Griffith Joyner, stretching the muscles is as important as strengthening them.

to shoulder level. The arms must never swing across the body nor the toes point outward. That could lose a valuable second.

During her daily training, Florence's husband, Al, watched her form, made suggestions on improving it, and massaged her legs at night. Most important, however, were his words of encouragement.

Florence Griffith Joyner was training as she had never trained before. "I really wanted to finish first in Rome in order to feel what it was like to be a winner," she said. "When you've been second best for so long, you can either accept it or try to become the best. I made the decision to try and be the best in 1988."

And now, 1988 had arrived.

The medalists in the women's 200-meter race in the 1984 Olympics held in Los Angeles (from left to right): U.S.A.'s Florence Griffith Joyner, silver medal; U.S.A.'s Valerie Brisco-Hooks, gold; and Jamaica's Merlene Ottey-Page, bronze

The 1988 U.S. Olympic team poses outside the
White House in Washington, D. C.

Chapter 4

IIIII THE OLYMPIC TRIALS

In 1988 the Olympics were held in Seoul, the capital of South Korea. For Florence Griffith Joyner and the other American athletes who made up the United States track and field team, the road to Seoul began in Indianapolis. That's where the U.S. Olympic track and field trials took place.

The trials, which began on July 15, lasted nine days and the Indiana University Track Stadium was packed each day with people watching the country's best athletes perform. The first day's attendance was nearly nine thousand.

On the second day, twenty-eight-year-old Griffith Joyner ran in the 100-meter heat. Heats are the first races in which runners are split into groups to compete against each other. In 1988, only three of the sprinters trying out for each event would finally make it onto the Olympic team. The experts who were predicting the outcome of the race didn't think Griffith Joyner would do that well—but they couldn't help but notice her. She was wearing a flashy green body-suit with one of its legs cut off. Nobody had run in an outfit like that before!

"On your mark."

Florence's hands were touching the ground, her thumbs just inside the starting line. The 98° F (36.7° C) temperature had made the track surface very hot.

"Set."

Bang!

The moment the gun was fired, Florence and the other sprinters took off.

Within seconds, Florence was ahead of every-one else—and she crossed the finish line with no one beside her. Her time was 10.60 seconds. Runner Evelyn Ashford's world record in 1984 was 10.76 seconds. Florence Griffith Joyner's time seemed like a world record, but the judges checked the wind speed meter.

There had been a wind (called a following wind or tail wind) of 3.2 meters per second, or 7.15 miles per hour, behind her and the other runners. Florence's time had not been a record-breaker after all. According to international rules, a following wind must not be more than

Florence Griffith Joyner competing in the 1988 Olympic trials

2 meters per second, or 4.47 miles per hour. So it must have been the wind that had pushed Florence and helped her run so fast!

Two and a half hours after her heat, Florence Griffith Joyner ran in a second race—called the quarterfinals—to try to earn a place on the Olympic team. She was wearing a turquoise and purple one-legged bodysuit; her fingernails were painted orange with black and white stripes at the ends.

Again, within seconds Florence was ahead of the other runners. As she neared the end of the race, she pushed her upper body forward so that her chest would hit the ribbon that stretched across the finish line. (It is the athlete whose torso—not arms or head—hits the ribbon first who wins.)

And again, the race was hers. The audience in the stadium was stunned. Florence Griffith Joyner had run 100 meters in 10.49 seconds. Some people hadn't even expected her to make it to the Olympic Games. Could this woman have made running history? Or was it the wind again that had helped her? The judges checked the wind gauge. It had not registered any wind! In the past twenty years, since racers' times have been measured electronically, the record for the

A jubilant Florence Griffith Joyner is lifted high in the air during the 1988 Olympic trials.

women's 100-meter dash had never been broken by more than 13/100ths of a second. Not only had Florence Griffith Joyner just run the 100-meter dash faster than any woman in history, she had also broken the record by 27/100ths of a second.

Suddenly, all the reporters from newspapers, magazines, and television stations wanted to talk to her. They started calling her "FloJo." The Flo was short for Florence (though it may also have been for her fluorescent bodysuits), the Jo for Joyner.

"When I saw the time," Florence told reporters after the event, "I couldn't believe it. But the 10.60 had made me realize I could get into the 10.50s. It made me realize if I kept concentrating, I could go faster."

The next day, Griffith Joyner won the semifinals in 10.70 seconds. A few hours later, wearing a fluorescent blue-and-white outfit, she raced in the finals against Evelyn Ashford. And Florence Griffith Joyner won again, finishing in 10.61 seconds.

Griffith Joyner's victories were not over. On the morning of July 23, she ran in the first heat for the 200-meter race. Twenty-six other women were competing against her—all had worked long and hard to reach this moment and their big chance to make it into the Olympic Games. But now, the attention of the crowd was focused on a new track star. Could Florence break yet another record?

It didn't look as if she could. Florence knew that in order to win, she couldn't be tense, that her arms and body had to be in just the right position, and that her strides had to be balanced.

As she ran, Florence knew she wasn't doing what she had spent years learning to do. She felt herself pushing too much, and her body wasn't properly balanced. When she got to the curve, she felt herself struggling. Florence crossed the finish line in 21.96 seconds. She had not been able to beat the record of her old friend Valerie Brisco, who had done it in 21.81 seconds four years earlier at the Olympic Games. Florence had come in second to her in that important race.

In the next race, the quarterfinals, Florence Griffith Joyner would run against Valerie, and all eyes in the stadium were on these two great sprinters.

"On your mark! Set!" *Bang!*

The runners burst from the blocks. Griffith Joyner's eyes were glued on the curve ahead. She knew she would need extra energy to overcome

Florence Griffith Joyner takes off from the
starting block in the 1988 Olympic trials.

the force of the bend. As she ran the curve, she leaned into it slightly. Her left shoulder was slightly forward to keep her from skidding.

Out of the corner of her eye, she could see Valerie running two lanes to her right. Within seconds, though, Florence passed her. She took the curve easily and then her upper body relaxed and her body straightened again as she went into the final straight path. And though she was running faster than any woman had before her, she didn't even seem to be pushing.

Florence Griffith Joyner didn't run across the finish line—she leaped across it. When she did, she also leaped into track history once again. She had just run the 200-meter in 21.77 seconds—setting a new American record! Brisco finished in 22. 36 seconds. The world record was 21.71, shared by two East German runners.

In her last race at the Indianapolis Trials, Florence wore an all-white lace bodysuit that she called an "athletic negligee." She finished in 21.85 seconds.

There was a disappointing side to the Olympic trials for Florence and her husband, Al Joyner. Al did not win a place on the American team in the triple jump. He told reporters that he wanted to try to make the 1992 Olympic team in the high hurdle.

After the race there was a press conference, in which reporters from newspapers, magazines, and TV stations asked questions of the winners.

One reporter asked Florence: "How did it feel?"

"Easy," she said.

"Can you run faster?" someone else asked.

"Yes," she said, without hesitation.

"The race was okay," she added. "I came to qualify for the Olympic Games and to stay healthy, and I accomplished that. I wanted to run the best curve of my life, and I feel when I run it strongly and relaxed, like I did today, I completed my purpose. Now I'm ready for my final goal, some Olympic gold."

Two months later, she would have the chance to prove herself.

Chapter 5

IIII THE OLYMPIC GAMES

Nearly 2,770 years ago, in 776 B.C. in Olympia, Greece, a group of men competed in what we usually call the first Olympic Games. (Many historians believe the games started even earlier.) There were racing, jumping, and throwing contests. The athletes competed in the nude. Women were not allowed to even watch the games, and the punishment for disobeying this rule was death. Greek women were allowed to compete among themselves, but their games had only a 500-foot run.

The winners of the Olympic Games had statues built in their honor, were the special guests at many parties, and didn't have to pay taxes for the rest of their lives.

The Olympic Games were abolished in 393 A.D. by the Roman emperor Theodosius, but they were started again in 1896 in Athens, Greece.

Opening ceremonies at the 1988
Olympics in Seoul, Korea

Once again, women were not allowed to compete—though they could watch! It was not until 1928 that women were finally allowed to participate in the Olympic Games. In that year they competed in five Olympic events in the Games held in Amsterdam, Holland.

In October, Florence Griffith Joyner and her husband and coach, Al Joyner, flew to Seoul, Korea, the site of the 1988 Olympic Games.

The trip did not start out well for Florence. Soon after they arrived at Seoul Airport, Al's baggage cart accidentally tipped over onto her left ankle, hurting her Achilles tendon. This is a large leg tendon that joins the muscles in the calf of the leg to the heel bone. Instead of training alongside the other athletes in the last few days before the Games, Florence was forced to rest. She put ice on the foot, stretched it, and prayed for it to heal. It did.

On the first day of the Games, Florence Griffith Joyner was ready to run.

Although there are forty-one track and field events in the Olympic Games, the 100-meter dash is one of the most exciting. Who will be named the fastest woman and the fastest man in the world? Will he or she beat the records of the last Olympic winners? If so, by how much? Griffith

Florence Griffith Joyner and her husband,
Al, being interviewed at the 1988 Olympics

Joyner would have three chances to win a gold medal—in the 100-meter, 200-meter, and relay races.

Seventy thousand people jammed into the stadium to watch the Games. When the gun went off for the 100-meter dash, all eyes were on the newest track star.

With tremendous force, Florence's front leg pushed against the block, and her back leg went forward and came up toward her chest. At the same time, one arm came forward and the other swung backward, helping to push her body forward. She came in at 10.88 seconds—beating Ashford's Olympic record of 10.97. In the quarterfinals, Florence beat the record again, coming in at 10.62.

In the semifinals, Florence Griffith Joyner was up against an even more powerful runner—5-feet 11-inch-tall East German Heike Drechsler. A few seconds after the runners left the blocks, though, the starter called the runners back. Florence had left the block a fraction of a second before the starter's gun had gone off. If she did it again, she would be disqualified from the race.

"On your mark. Set." *Bang!*

This time, Florence was more careful—almost too careful. She took off slowly and Drechsler was quick to get ahead of her. But at 50 meters, Florence surged ahead. She came across the finish line smiling at 10.70—21/100ths of a second ahead of Drechsler.

Florence Griffith Joyner still had to run in the finals of the 100-meter dash. Once again, she would run against the great runners Ashford and Drechsler. All three bolted from the blocks at the sound of the gun. But Florence moved ahead of the others almost immediately and never let them take the lead. At 90 meters a huge smile appeared on Florence Griffith Joyner's face, and by 95 meters she had raised her arms in victory. At that moment, Florence knew everything had been worth it. She completed the race in 10.54 seconds! (Because of a tail wind, it would not be her official record time.) Ashford, who came in second, was a distant 10.83.

Florence Griffith Joyner had achieved the dream of a lifetime—an Olympic gold medal.

Three days later, on September 28, Griffith Joyner was on the field again, competing in the 200-meter race.

In the semifinals, she broke the world record of 21.71 by finishing in 21.56 seconds. In the final race, two hours later, Florence Griffith Joyner wanted to do even better. To do so, she would

Florence Griffith Joyner raises her arms in victory as she wins the women's 100-meter final at the Seoul Olympics. Her time of 10.54 seconds broke her own record.

need to use all she had learned about sprinting and her own body's abilities in the past twenty years. But in those brief seconds, she wouldn't have time to think about those lessons. They would have to come to her as naturally as the way she breathed. If they didn't, another woman would be feeling the pride and excitement of being number one.

"On your mark. Set." *Bang!*

Florence Griffith Joyner took off. As she ran, thoughts speeded through her head. *Don't start too fast. It will use up too much energy you'll need to overcome the force of the bend.*

She rounded the bend. *Keep your left shoulder slightly forward to keep from skidding. Keep the upper body relaxed and hug the inside of the lane.*

Florence was back on the straight path and nearing the finish line. *Remember! Use all you have coming home.*

Florence Griffith Joyner crossed the finish line in an astonishing 21.34 seconds—beating her own record that she had just set!

When she saw the time, Griffith Joyner kneeled on the track in sheer joy, her hands clasped together, her head bowed. Al Joyner ran

An emotional Florence after winning the 200-meter gold medal

onto the field, hugged his wife, and whirled her around.

Griffith Joyner had won her second gold, but she had not finished running. Two days later, on October 1, she ran in the relays. In the 4 × 400-meter relay, each runner runs the 400 meters around the track before passing the baton, a hollow piece of wood or metal, to the next runner in the "exchange zone." In the 4 × 100-meter relay, each runner runs 100 meters around the track. Passing the baton is not easy. The runners must be running at the same speed and they cannot bump into each other. It takes a lot of practice. If the baton falls, only the person handing it over may pick it up.

Griffith Joyner was denied entrance on an Olympic relay team in 1984 because officials said her nails were too long to pass the baton. In 1988 Griffith Joyner was allowed to run.

In the 4 × 100 women's relay, Griffith Joyner's pass to Evelyn Ashford, who was running the final leg, was shaky and she almost dropped it, but Griffith Joyner went on to win the gold for the American team—by 3 feet!

Just forty minutes later, Griffith Joyner ran the 1,600-meter relay—though she had not been

Florence Griffith Joyner runs with the baton in
the women's 4 × 400-meter race.

training to run such a distance. She ran the final leg in 48.1 seconds, helping the U.S. women's team break a world record. But the Soviet Union's team also broke the world record in that race, with an even better time, so they beat the American team nonetheless. However, Griffith Joyner came in only 2 meters behind the Soviet runner.

The 1988 Olympic Games were over. Florence Griffith Joyner had won three gold medals and one silver medal.

"It was more than I ever dreamed of," said Florence, tired but proud. "I'm so happy."

A few months later, in Portland, Oregon, the U.S. Olympics Committee honored Florence Griffith Joyner as the female athlete of the year. She cried when she received the award. In New York a few days later, she accepted the Jesse Owens Award as 1988's outstanding track and field athlete.

On February 25, 1989, Florence Griffith Joyner announced her retirement, saying she wanted to spend more time writing books for children and acting. Since then, she has given birth to a baby. She lives with her family in Van Nuys, California.

Florence exhibits both her 1988 Olympic medals
—three gold and one silver—and her fingernails.

Holding her nephew, Jason, Florence is greeted
by relatives upon her return home from the 1988
Olympics. To the left is her husband, Al Joyner, and
to the right is her mother, Florence Griffith.

Florence recently said that she plans to return to sprinting and to run in another Olympics. Her fans, sports lovers, and the millions of people who have been amazed by this extraordinary woman's talents are eagerly awaiting her return.

For Further Reading

Arnold, Caroline. *The Olympic Summer Games*. New York: Franklin Watts, 1991.

Bourgeois, Paulette. *On Your Mark, Get Set: All About the Olympics Then and Now*. Toronto: Kids Can Press, 1987.

Gleasner, Diana C. *Women in Sports: Track and Field*. New York: Harvey House, 1977.

Rosen, Mel and Karen Rosen. *Sports Illustrated Track: Championship Running*. New York: Time, Inc., 1988.

Index

Ashford, Evelyn, 38, 42, 51, 52, 56
Athens, Greece, 47

Boston Marathon, 1967, 10
Brisco, Valerie, 22, 43, 45

California State University, 21

Drechsler, Heike, 51–52

False starts, 17–19, 51
Following winds, 19, 38–40, 52

Gold medals, Olympic, 52, 56
Griffith, Delorez Florence. *See* Joyner, Florence Griffith
Griffith, Florence, 10–11
Griffith, Robert, 10–11

Indiana University Track Stadium, 37

Jesse Owens Award, 58
Jordan High School, 14
Joyner, Alfrederick Alphonzo, 25, 35, 45–46, 49, 54–55

Joyner, Florence Griffith:
    early life, 9–14
    marriage, 25
    Olympic games,
      1988, 49–59
    Olympic trials,
      1988, 37–46
    retirement, 58–59
    training, 21–31
Joyner-Kersee, Jackie, 25

Kersee, Bobby, 21, 25, 26

Los Angeles, California, 22

Moscow, USSR, 25

National Collegiate Athletic Association, 22

Olympia, Greece, 47
Olympic games:
    history of, 47–48

1980, 25
1984, 22, 25
1988, 10, 49–59
One-hundred-meter races, 15–20

Relay races, 56–57

Seoul, South Korea, 10, 37, 49
Silver medal, Olympic, 58
Sprinters, 15
Sugar Ray Robinson Youth Foundation, 12

Theodosius, 47
Track events, 15–20
Two-hundred-meter races, 20

United States Olympics Committee, 58
University of California at Los Angeles, 21, 22

Van Nuys, California, 58